Alive in the WORD

CLOUD OF WITNESSES

I0792876

BARNABAS

Man for Others

Jerome Kodell

Little Rock Scripture Study

A ministry of the Diocese of Little Rock
in partnership with Liturgical Press

Nihil obstat: Msgr. Francis I. Malone, *Censor Librorum.*
Imprimatur: ✠ Anthony B. Taylor, Bishop of Little Rock, November 17, 2017.

Cover design by Ann Blattner. Cover photo: Getty Images. Used with permission.

Photos/illustrations: Page 6, *St. Barnabas and St. Paul*, Cyprus. Courtesy of Wikimedia Commons. Page 13, *Saint Paul Preaching*, mosaic. Courtesy of Wikimedia Commons. Page 17, Icon of Saint Barnabas, Museum of St. Barnabas Salamis, Cyprus. Courtesy of Wikimedia Commons. Page 19, *Peter Baptizing the Centurion Cornelius* by Francesco Treuisani, 1709. Courtesy of Wikimedia Commons. Page 21, map by Ann Blattner. Pages 29 and 33, Getty Images. Used with permission. Page 36, Goodsalt.com. Used with permission. Page 38, *Saint Barnabas* by Angelica Kaufmann. Courtesy of Wikimedia Commons.

ISBN: 978-0-8146-4456-0 (print); 978-0-8146-4480-5 (ebook)

Contents

Introduction

Alive in the Word brings you resources to deepen your understanding of Scripture, offer meaning for your life today, and help you to pray and act in response to God's word.

Use any volume of **Alive in the Word** in the way best suited to you.

- **For individual learning and reflection,** consider this an invitation to prayerfully journal in response to the questions you find along the way. And be prepared to move from head to heart and then to action.
- **For group learning and reflection,** arrange for three sessions where you will use the material provided as the basis for faith sharing and prayer. You may ask group members to read each chapter in advance and come prepared with questions answered. In this kind of session, plan to be together for about an hour. Or, if your group prefers, read and respond to the questions together without advance preparation. With this approach, it's helpful to plan on spending more time for each group session in order to adequately work through each of the chapters.

- **For a parish-wide event** or use within a larger group, provide each person with a copy of this volume, and allow time during the day for quiet reading, group discussion and prayer, and then a final commitment by each person to some simple action in response to what he or she learned.

This volume on the topic of Barnabas is one of several volumes dedicated to **Cloud of Witnesses**. The pages of our Bibles are filled with the stories of women and men who have played a unique role in salvation history. By entering into a few key biblical passages written by or describing these people, we begin to see how our own story continues God's great work of salvation in the world. Their witness, handed on to us from centuries ago, continues to speak to us and challenge us to stand as faithful witnesses in today's world.

Barnabas and Saul: The Beginning

Begin by asking God to assist you in your prayer and study. Then slowly read through a brief passage from Acts 9, which describes the first encounter between Barnabas and Saul.

Acts 9:26-30
[26]When [Saul] arrived in Jerusalem he tried to join the dis-
ciples, but they were all afraid of him, not believing that he
was a disciple. [27]Then Barnabas took charge of him and
brought him to the apostles, and he reported to them how
on the way he had seen the Lord and that he had spoken to
him, and how in Damascus he had spoken out boldly in the
name of Jesus. [28]He moved about freely with them in Jeru-
salem, and spoke out boldly in the name of Jesus. [29]He also
spoke and debated with the Hellenists, but they tried to kill
him. [30]And when the brothers learned of this, they took him
down to Caesarea and sent him on his way to Tarsus.

After a few moments of quiet reflection on the scene described in Acts 9, consider the following background information provided in Setting the Scene. The occasional questions in the margins may be used for your own reflection and/or for group discussion.

Setting the Scene

Saul and Barnabas come together in the narrative of the Acts of the Apostles here for the first time, but we have been introduced to them before. We met Barnabas first, when he was presented as a model member of the Christian community in Jerusalem, having sold his property and given the money to the apostles to help the needy (Acts 4:36-37). We also learned that his given name was Joseph, and that Barnabas was an Aramaic nickname given to him by the apostles, rendered in Greek as "son of encouragement" or "son of consolation." He was a native of the island of Cyprus and a member of a Jewish Levite family. Besides the identity revealed in his nickname, we learn that he is a Hellenist Christian (one born and raised in a Greek-speaking community outside of Israel), that he is therefore considered an immigrant (potentially an outsider) in Jerusalem, and that he was raised in an observant Jewish family, probably speaking Hebrew at home. All of this will have significance as the story in Acts unfolds.

How does the meaning of the name "Barnabas" create expectations about the plot of the story?

One of Luke's favorite words in his gospel and in the Acts of the Apostles is the Greek *dei*, "it is (or was) necessary," in the sense of divine destiny or providence: "Did you not know that

I must be [*dei*] in my Father's house?" (Luke 2:49); "the Son of Man must be [*dei*] handed over to sinners and be crucified" (24:7); "Was it not necessary that the Messiah should suffer these things and enter into his glory?" (24:26); "It is necessary for us to undergo many hardships to enter the kingdom of God" (Acts 14:22); "the Messiah had to [*dei*] suffer and rise from the dead" (17:3). In his introduction of Barnabas, Luke implies divine providence at work, for already from his birth the young man is being prepared for the special role he will play in the development of the Christian church.

Our first notice of Saul was as a young man who witnessed the stoning of Stephen with approval (Acts 7:58; 8:1). The next we heard of him he was "breathing murderous threats against the disciples of the Lord" and seeking authorization to persecute Christians in Damascus (9:1-2). On the way there, he had the momentous revelation of Jesus Christ that turned him from a persecutor to an avid disciple, and heard the voice from heaven asking, "Saul, Saul, why are you persecuting me?" (9:4). Of this experience he later wrote to the Galatians, "[God], who from my mother's womb had set me apart and called me through his grace, was pleased to reveal his Son to me, so that I might proclaim him to the Gentiles" (Gal 1:15-16). Instead of entering Damascus as a persecutor, he came as a Christian preacher proclaiming that Jesus is the Son of God and the Messiah, but he spoke in such a fiery and challenging way that he aroused the hostility of the Jews, who conspired to kill him.

When we meet him in the present episode with Barnabas, Saul has just had a daring escape from Damascus, having been lowered through an opening in the city wall in a basket by his friends (Acts 9:25). The apostle himself later writes about this in 2 Corinthians, specifying that it was the local ruler, the governor under King Aretas (11:32), who ordered the city sealed to prevent his escape. This information permits us, with the help of extra-biblical sources, to date the escape and Saul's arrival in Jerusalem to the year 38 or 39.

Saul, like Barnabas, had been providentially prepared for the role he would play in the Gentile mission. He was also a Hellenist, born in Tarsus in Asia Minor (modern Turkey), and raised in a devout Jewish family who sent him to Jerusalem to study as early as age twelve under Rabbi Gamaliel (Acts 22:3). Thus, he was at home in both Hebrew and Greek cultures and was, in addition, well-trained in Jewish Scripture and theology.

Acts 9:26-30 will be explored a few verses at a time to deepen your understanding and appreciation.

Understanding the Scene Itself

26When [Saul] arrived in Jerusalem he tried to join the disciples, but they were all afraid of him, not believing that he was a disciple. 27Then Barnabas took charge of him and brought him to the

apostles, and he reported to them how on the way he had seen the Lord and that he had spoken to him, and how in Damascus he had spoken out boldly in the name of Jesus.

It is understandable that the disciples in Jerusalem would have been suspicious of Saul's intentions. They had known him only as the arch persecutor who had approved of Stephen's martyrdom, the event that sparked the flight of Greek-speaking Christians from Jerusalem (Acts 8:1), and they had seen him depart for Damascus on a mission to arrest Christians and bring them back in chains (9:2). Now they are expected to embrace him as a brother. They feared that he might be an infiltrator posing as a Christian who could get them arrested or killed.

When has someone's reputation prevented you from trusting or taking seriously their message?

Barnabas takes the initiative, which will eventually, though not immediately, bring Saul into the forefront of the Christian mission to the Gentiles and, along with his letters in the New Testament, have a lasting impact on the history of the church. He "takes charge" of Saul and introduces him to the leadership of the Jerusalem church, giving him a chance to tell his story and to be accepted into the community and begin preaching in the name of Jesus.

We begin to understand in this episode why Barnabas made such an impression as a helper and promoter of others that the Hebrew leaders named him the "son of encouragement." Like Simon who became Peter, Joseph of Cyprus would become so identified by his reputation as "Barnabas the encourager" that his given name

BARNABAS "son of encouragement"

was virtually forgotten (see 1 Cor 9:6; Gal 2:1, 9, 13; Col 4:10). That he is still remembered this way without any demurral long after his death attests to the genuineness and consistency of his reputation. Here he goes out of his way at some personal risk to come to the aid of the dangerous Saul so that he will have a chance to prove himself to the apostles.

Any member of the Jerusalem community would have been at risk in promoting Saul, a still unknown (and potentially explosive) quantity, but there were added dimensions to the risk for Barnabas, who had more to lose in worldly terms. Barnabas was the only "outsider" in the core group of leaders in the Jerusalem community. All of the rest of the Jerusalem leaders we know by name in Acts—Peter, John, James his brother and James the "brother of the Lord," Judas Barsabbas, and Silas—were natives of Israel, but Barnabas was from Greek-speaking Cyprus. He was apparently completely bilingual, having been brought up in the Greek culture but in a fervent Hebrew-speaking Jewish family, but it would have been extremely rare and unlikely

In what ways does an "outsider" status sometimes benefit a situation and sometimes not?

for one of his background to become so trusted and embedded in the Jerusalem leadership. It is a sign of the trust placed in him by the Hebrew leadership that they would accept Saul into fellowship simply at Barnabas' word.

We know from several references in the early chapters of Acts that there was a natural division between Hebrew-speaking Christians and Greek-speaking Christians. Earlier in the story, "the Hellenists complained against the Hebrews because their widows were being neglected in the daily distribution" (Acts 6:1). This was apparently an oversight quickly remedied by the Hebrew-speaking leaders. As is often the case, the immigrant men learned the local language first because of their work in public, but the women typically stayed at home and often had no need to speak the new language. When their husbands died, this left them isolated and unable to get the help they needed without the intervention of others. They didn't know where to turn.

When have you seen Christians treat one another differently because of their cultural or ethnic backgrounds?

We know that the Jewish community viewed the Hebrew and Greek Christians as two different groups, because in the wake of the martyrdom of the Hellenist Stephen, it was only the Greek-speaking Christians who were forced to flee Jerusalem. It is striking that Barnabas was able to remain, an indication of how strongly he was identified with the Hebrew leadership inside and outside the community.

For Barnabas to take a chance on Saul was also to risk his own reputation and his enviable position in the heart of the Jerusalem Church. There is no indication that this danger entered

Barnabas' mind; this is the first of several instances when he seemed to have given no thought for his own benefit but only for the good of others and the church.

**28He moved about freely with them in Jerusalem,
and spoke out boldly in the name of Jesus. 29He
also spoke and debated with the Hellenists, but
they tried to kill him. 30And when the brothers
learned of this, they took him down to Caesarea
and sent him on his way to Tarsus.**

Just as he had in Damascus, Saul "spoke out boldly" in the name of the Lord in Jerusalem. And just as before, his boldness got him into trouble. This would not be the last time. Saul was not known for diplomacy. When later during the successful preaching mission at Antioch in Pisidia (Acts 13:13-43) his activity aroused the hostility of a group of Jews there, he did not dialogue with them, but told them that they were rejecting the word of God and condemning

themselves as unworthy of eternal life (13:46). Not surprisingly, this caused his listeners to incite a persecution against him and Barnabas, and they were expelled from the territory (13:50). Later, some of the offended party would follow them to Lystra and stone Saul, leaving him for dead (14:19).

We should not be startled, then, knowing this would happen in the future and remembering the experience that forced his escape from Damascus, that his abrasive language aroused the hostility of the Hellenists in Jerusalem (meaning here the Jews who had moved to Israel from Greek-speaking countries). Like Barnabas, Saul was a Hellenist himself, having grown up in Tarsus in Asia Minor (modern Turkey), and was also apparently completely bilingual. It was probably particularly galling to these Jews that one of their own was speaking so forcefully about Jesus as the Messiah. We can imagine a shouting match rather than a calm exchange of ideas. At any rate, Saul's preaching had the same effect as it had in Damascus, inspiring not conversion but a desire to kill him.

Can you recall any instances when the style of delivery of a message overshadowed the message itself? Is there some wisdom here about one's tone and demeanor?

The Christian leaders had already had enough to deal with in the earlier persecution because of Stephen and they could not afford to have Saul raise the heat again. As much as they might have recognized his strong faith and his preaching ability, for the sake of the mission at this time they had to send him on his way. They took him to the seaport of Caesarea and put him on a boat for Tarsus, his hometown. They probably did not expect to see him again.

> **Without the initiative taken by Barnabas, we might never have heard of Saul.**

There is a certain ironic humor in the very next sentence in Luke's account after Saul's departure: "The church throughout all Judea, Galilee, and Samaria was at peace" (Acts 9:31). We will not hear of Saul again until Barnabas goes to Tarsus to retrieve him years later. Without Barnabas' initiative, we might never have heard of Saul. He had apparently settled down in Tarsus to his trade, sewing together the hides of goats for making tents (Acts 18:3). It is unlikely that he remained silent about Jesus during this time, though we have no information about a preaching mission in Tarsus.

Praying the Word / Sacred Reading

If you had been in the area of Damascus or Jerusalem after Saul's conversion, would you have been leery of trusting him? Would it have made a difference to have the testimony of a trusted leader like Barnabas?

Use your people, Lord, to lead us in your direction.
Send us as witnesses who have experienced your love and truth and beauty.
This week we pray in thanksgiving for others who speak on your behalf, especially __________ [provide names].
When opportunities arise, help each of us to speak convincingly and sincerely of your work in our lives.

Living the Word

Consider the official and unofficial leaders within your own faith community. Does their witness, invitation, and/or encouragement tend to draw you to participate in an event or project or faith formation opportunity? Take time soon to thank these people for being encouraging leaders.

Ask God to provide you with opportunities to speak up for others too.

Barnabas Risks Again

Begin by asking God to assist you in your prayer and study. Then slowly read through the following passage from Acts 11, which recounts how Barnabas "recruited" Saul for the mission in Antioch.

Acts 11:19-26

**19Now those who had been scattered
by the persecution that arose because
of Stephen went as far as Phoenicia,
Cyprus, and Antioch, preaching the
word to no one but Jews. 20There were
some Cypriots and Cyrenians among
them, however, who came to Antioch
and began to speak to the Greeks as
well, proclaiming the Lord Jesus. 21The hand of the Lord was
with them and a great number who believed turned to the
Lord. 22The news about them reached the ears of the church
in Jerusalem, and they sent Barnabas [to go] to Antioch.
23When he arrived and saw the grace of God, he rejoiced and
encouraged them all to remain faithful to the Lord in firmness
of heart, 24for he was a good man, filled with the holy Spirit
and faith. And a large number of people was added to the
Lord. 25Then he went to Tarsus to look for Saul, 26and when
he had found him he brought him to Antioch. For a whole**

year they met with the church and taught a large number of people, and it was in Antioch that the disciples were first called Christians.

After a few moments of quiet reflection on the scene described in Acts 11, gain a fuller understanding of the context by reading Setting the Scene. Questions in the margin continue for your personal use or for group discussion.

Setting the Scene

We do not know how much time passed between Saul's departure from Jerusalem to Tarsus and his arrival in Antioch to join the Christian mission at the invitation of Barnabas. The respected Bible scholar Fr. Joseph Fitzmyer, SJ, suggests the period 40–44. We are told that the Christian community in Antioch had been founded by refugees from the persecution aroused by Stephen's death (Acts 7:54-60), which is dated to the mid-30s, so the church had been developing there for eight to ten years before the events narrated in this passage.

We get a glimpse here of one of the most divisive issues to exercise the early Christian church: whether or not non-Jews could be admitted to the community directly, without some Jewish initiation and observance. Luke is gradually working his way to the decision of the Council of Jerusalem as recounted in Acts 15, which affirmed that membership would from then on be open to all without restriction. But this was not easy. According to Acts 2, all those who received the Spirit at Pentecost were either Jews by birth or convert Jews, and the apostles did not have a clear mandate from Jesus on the question of expanding the mission, though there were apparently scattered initiatives to incorporate Gentiles. Just prior to the present account, Luke had related the story of the baptism of the Gentile Cornelius by Peter in Caesarea (Acts 10:1-48; 11:1-18), but whether it happened before or after Antioch is not clear.

Earlier, Luke had recounted a mission with parallels to the one in Antioch when Philip, one of the seven Hellenist leaders (Acts 6:5), fled north to Samaria after Stephen's martyrdom and began a successful preaching ministry there. The Jerusalem leaders did not know whether the baptism of Samaritans was justified, so they sent Peter and John to investigate. Jesus himself had had some positive contacts with Samaritans, with the grateful leper he had healed (Luke 17:11-19) and with the woman at the well and her townspeople (John 4:39-42), and had preached the parable of the Good Samaritan (Luke 10:29-37), so the apostles were open to good possibilities. When the Holy Spirit came down upon the Samaritans, the apostles recognized that the development was of God and they returned with the news to Jerusalem, preaching in Samaritan villages along the way (8:4-25).

The apostles could not trust this experience as a mandate for a wide-open Gentile mission in Antioch, for the Samaritans had a Jewish heritage, spoke Hebrew, and were not considered Gentiles as such. But the situation in Antioch was especially touchy because of the issue of language and culture. Peter and John could be trusted by the Samaritans to make a fair judgment because they shared the same language and basic culture. And their decision, even if some disagreed with it, could be accepted by the conservative Hebrew Christians in Jerusalem.

But Peter and John could not perform the same service for Antioch. The Greek-speaking community there might be suspicious if the verdict were negative, and the Hebrew-speaking community in Jerusalem might be suspicious if it were positive. Either side could complain that because of the language and culture divide, Peter and John had not really understood what was going on. By God's providence the leaders could call on Barnabas, a Hellenist himself but also a respected and trusted member of the Jerusalem leadership, completely bilingual and at home in both cultures.

How might a common cultural or ethnic heritage provide a bridge in difficult situations today?

Acts 11:19-26 will be explored a few verses at a time to deepen your understanding and appreciation.

Understanding the Scene Itself

19Now those who had been scattered by the persecution that arose because of Stephen went as far as Phoenicia, Cyprus, and Antioch, preaching

the word to no one but Jews. [20]There were some Cypriots and Cyrenians among them, however, who came to Antioch and began to speak to the Greeks as well, proclaiming the Lord Jesus. [21]The hand of the Lord was with them and a great number who believed turned to the Lord.

In the flight from Jerusalem, Christian missionaries fanned out north and west. The presence of Cyprus and Cypriots will be important for the assignment of the Cypriot Barnabas. At first the Christian mission had been only to the Jews, but eventually Cypriots and Cyrenians began to preach to the Greeks.

Mention is made of Phoenicia and of Cyrenians, but with no further explanation. Phoenicia is the territory to the northwest of Israel along the seacoast in what are now the countries of Lebanon and Syria. The chief ancient cities Tyre and Sidon are often mentioned in the Old Testament. Jesus ministered there and healed a Syrophoenician woman's child (Mark 7:24-30). Though the people of the region were pagans, they came to listen to Jesus (3:8). That the Gospel took root there and flourished early is illustrated by the stopover there by Paul when he was on his way from Ephesus to Rome on his third missionary journey: "There we sought out the disciples and stayed for a week" (Acts 21:4). A strong Christian community continues to exist in the

region to this day, especially in the form of Maronite and Melkite Churches.

Cyrene, in modern-day Libya, had been home to a large Jewish community for a long time. A Jerusalem synagogue formed of Cyrenians and other Hellenist Jews is mentioned in the account of the debate with Stephen (Acts 6:9), and we know of Simon of Cyrene, a Jew in Jerusalem for the Passover, who was conscripted to help Jesus carry the cross to Calvary. When this is mentioned in the Gospel of Mark, the point is made that Simon was the father of Alexander and Rufus (Mark 15:21). This must mean that by the time of the writing of the gospel, Alexander and Rufus were known to the readers as Christians. The Christian Gospel arrived in Cyrene early, and one of the members of the Antioch community that sent Barnabas and Saul on their first mission was Lucius of Cyrene (Acts 13:1).

What does it tell you about the commitment and convictions of the early Christian missionaries that the Good News spread so far and so rapidly?

The point is made that the Cypriots and Cyrenians were proclaiming the Lord Jesus. In Samaria, Philip had proclaimed Jesus as the Messiah (Acts 8:5), and in Damascus, Saul had preached Jesus as both the Son of God and the Messiah (9:20, 22). These are not idle distinctions. Jesus as Lord or the Son of God was a concept understandable in a Greek culture that spoke of God as Lord (*kurios*) and had many gods and sons of gods, but Gentiles would not have understood or been interested in Jesus as Messiah. On the other hand, a Jewish audience would have known all about the Messiah, which was the focus of their expectation, but to speak of Jesus as Lord or Son of God could have been taken by them as the blasphemous idea that Jesus was personally the God of the Hebrew Scriptures. We see here an indication that the preachers tailored their message to their audiences, preaching Jesus first as either Messiah or Lord depending on the background of their listeners, and then later, when interest was aroused and there was an opening, completing the proclamation.

When and how has a homilist's awareness of his audience and their circumstances enhanced a homily?

In saying that "a great number who believed turned to the Lord," Luke is implying by use of terminology that the same thing is happening in this Gentile territory that took place in the early days in Jerusalem: "And every day the Lord added to their number those who were being saved" (Acts 2:47); "Yet more than ever, believers in the Lord, great numbers of men and women, were added to them" (5:14).

22The news about them reached the ears of the church in Jerusalem, and they sent Barnabas [to go] to Antioch. 23When he arrived and saw the grace of God, he rejoiced and encouraged them all to remain faithful in the Lord and in firmness of heart, 24for he was a good man, filled with the holy Spirit and faith. And a large number of people was added to the Lord.

We can imagine that a large amount of discussion, debate, and prayer is camouflaged by that first sentence: they heard the news and they sent Barnabas. The expression "reached the ears" implies that the report was not direct, and perhaps people were hesitant to tell the Jerusalem leaders what was going on in Antioch. When it did reach the leaders, it probably aroused a good measure of anxiety. Is this proper? Is this legitimate? Do we have the authority to allow or approve the incorporation of Gentiles without any Jewish background into the church? And then, if we need to send someone to investigate, who could it be? We have seen the potential problems posed by the barriers of language and culture.

Barnabas was chosen for the mission: a Hellenist acceptable to the Hebrews, a man trusted by both sides. But there is more to his qualifications than that, as Luke implies by his terminology. He "saw the grace of God." He was able to see the potential beyond the immediate barriers, as he had seen beyond the problems of Saul's initial conduct as a Christian preacher to his potential for the church in the long run. The grace Barnabas saw had been at work from the foundation days of the Christian community in Jerusalem: "With great power the apostles bore witness to the resurrection of the Lord Jesus, and great favor was accorded them all" (literally, "great grace was upon them all"; Acts 4:33). He perceived the grace of God working in a new way in Antioch.

Sometimes God's grace urges us to see a bigger picture and work toward a more long-term goal. When has this been your experience of grace?

Barnabas is "filled with faith and the holy Spirit" as was Stephen (6:5); and both of them are reflections of Jesus himself, who was filled "with the holy Spirit and power" (10:38). Luke is implying that this is a continuation of the work of the Holy Spirit, who has been guiding events in the mission of Jesus and the growth of the church since the annunciation of Jesus' birth at the beginning of the gospel (Luke 1:35).

Barnabas' reaction to this action of God is a play on his nickname: he "*encouraged* them all to remain faithful in the Lord." The Greek word for "encouragement" or "consolation," *paraklesis*, has a strong pedigree in the New Testament, being the focus of a moving meditation at the beginning of Paul's Second Letter to the Corinthians (1:3-7), where forms of the word appear ten times in five verses; and in Johannine theology, Paraclete is the name of the Holy Spirit (John 14:16, 26; 15:26; 16:7) and of Jesus himself (1 John 2:1).

> The Greek word for "encouragement" or "consolation" is *paraklesis*.

The sending of Barnabas meant a complete change in his life, a wrenching away from his comfortable nest in the Jerusalem community, where he had prestige and clout as a member of the inner core of authority. He will go to Antioch, an unknown territory where he has no contacts, and never return to live in Jerusalem. Here again there is no indication that Barnabas gave his personal loss a second thought. He was completely available for the church's mission, wherever his help was required.

When has God's grace met with resistance in your life? What fears might be part of resisting God's call?

Here and in Acts 5:14, when people are baptized, Luke doesn't say only that they became members of the community, but that by joining the group of disciples, they were "added to the Lord." The identity of the community as the body of the Lord is emphasized in the story of Ananias and Sapphira, who, when they were dishonest to Peter as head of the church, were told, "You have lied not to human beings, but to God" (5:4); and in the experience of Saul on his way to arrest Christians in Damascus when he heard Jesus ask him, "Saul, why are you persecuting me?" (9:4).

25Then he went to Tarsus to look for Saul, 26and when he found him he brought him to Antioch. For a whole year they met with the church and taught a large number of people, and it was in Antioch that the disciples were first called Christians.

Though Saul's first attempts at proclaiming the Christian Gospel had not been successful and even had alarming effects, Barnabas had seen something in Saul that he felt held great promise. This proved to be a decisive insight for the church. There is probably much unsaid behind Luke's laconic statement that "when he found him he brought him to Antioch." Saul was not easygoing and may still have been smarting from his treatment in Jerusalem. Barnabas probably had to exercise all his tact in convincing Saul to join him in Antioch and to reassure him that the result would be better this time. We also recognize again Barnabas' commitment to do what he judged best for the Christian mission, whatever it might cost him personally. He probably sensed that Saul had the ability, if properly directed, to become the prominent partner in

Do you see in someone else a gift that could be developed? How might you encourage that person?

their team and to put Barnabas in the background, which is exactly what would happen. He also may have foreseen that working with the irascible and impetuous Saul would create some times of awkwardness and stress for him.

Luke tells us that it was in Antioch that the disciples of Jesus were first called Christians. Away from Jerusalem the community was able to be discerned as no longer just a sect of Judaism but a separate entity, and their recognition of Jesus as the Messiah was enshrined permanently in the Greek form of Messiah, *Christos*, in the community's name.

The recognition of Jesus as the Messiah was enshrined permanently in the Greek form of Messiah, *Christos,* in the community's name: CHRISTIAN.

Praying the Word / Sacred Reading

When Barnabas arrived in Antioch he "saw the grace of God." God's grace is more than simply a feeling—it is visible, tangible, and possesses God's very transformative power.

Where do you "see the grace of God" in your life? In your family life? In your work? In your community? How does this "seeing" transform you?

O God, you gave Barnabas the gift of
seeing your work among your people.
May I have such vision.

You gave Barnabas the gift of joy and
encouragement to grow the faith of
others.
May your work among us give me such joy.

You gave Barnabas the guidance of your
Spirit to provide for the needs of your
people.
May I respond to your Spirit in the same
selfless way.

Living the Word

Who among you needs some encouragement and leadership in order to grow? What projects could benefit from the attention and assistance of other skilled people? How could you help facilitate this? Are you willing to be a Barnabas figure in your corner of the world?

The Cost of Discipleship

Once again, ask God to assist you in your prayer and study. Then slowly read through the following passage from Acts 15, which recalls the tension that arose between Barnabas and Paul.

Acts 15:36-40

36After some time Paul said to Barnabas, "Come, let us make
a return visit to see how the brothers are getting on in all the
cities where we proclaimed the word of the Lord." 37Barnabas
wanted to take with them also John, who was called Mark.
38But Paul insisted that they should not take with them some-
one who had deserted them at Pamphylia and who had not
continued with them in their work. 39So sharp was their dis-
agreement that they separated. Barnabas took Mark and
sailed to Cyprus. 40But Paul chose Silas and departed after
being commended by the brothers to the grace of the Lord.

After a few moments of quiet reflection on the passage, consider the information provided in Setting the Scene.

Setting the Scene

In the previous episode, Barnabas and Saul were at Antioch, just beginning their partnership together for the Gospel. At this point, as much as three years have passed (46–49) while they completed a preaching mission throughout Asia Minor and returned to spend "no little time" in Antioch (Acts 14:28) before they came to Jerusalem for the momentous council. In the meantime, Saul had begun to use the Greek or Roman form of his name, Paul. Now, after the council, they come to a parting of ways. Our sadness and disappointment at this split is tempered by the later references in 1 Corinthians 9:6, Colossians 4:10, and Philemon 24 that imply Paul has been reconciled to both Barnabas and Mark. But this glimpse into the life of the early missionaries shows that the pressures of relationship, even among disciples with the best motives, have been there from the beginning.

A new figure is introduced here, John, "who is called Mark" (Acts 12:12), identified as the cousin of Barnabas in Colossians 4:10. He accompanied Barnabas and Saul when they set out from Antioch to Cyprus on their first missionary journey (Acts 13:4-5). They must have been nervous on this first attempt to carry the Gospel to new territory, but their positive experience gave them the courage to decide to go on from Cyprus to Pamphylia on the mainland of Asia Minor. But at this point, John Mark left them and returned to Jerusalem, an action that became the source of the later quarrel.

There is a subtle shift in language to indicate that Saul, now called Paul, is becoming the leader of the mission. When they set out from Antioch, Barnabas was listed first in the group of prophets and teachers, and Saul last (13:1-2), but by the time they head for Pamphylia, it is "Paul and his companions" who set sail (13:13). Again, there is no indication of any struggle or disagreement on Barnabas' part that Paul should take over if that were best for the mission.

Paul was obviously still vexed at this later date by what he saw as John Mark's desertion in Cyprus and would not consent to the young man's presence on their new mission. As a result, Paul and Barnabas part ways, Barnabas sailing to Cyprus with Mark, and Paul returning with Silas to the towns in Asia Minor he and Barnabas had evangelized earlier. The providential outcome of this unfortunate quarrel was to double the preaching mission.

> *Acts 15:36-40 will be explored a few verses at a time to deepen your understanding and appreciation.*

Understanding the Scene Itself

36After some time Paul said to Barnabas, "Come, let us make a return visit to see how the brothers are getting on in all the cities where we proclaimed the word of the Lord."

This scene takes place after a watershed moment in the history of the early church, a decision that validated the course Paul and Barnabas had taken and set in motion a new era of evangelization to the nations.

Centuries after the era of Paul and Barnabas, we may take for granted the universal nature of the church. How do the struggles of the early church instruct or encourage us today?

Luke pictures the debate about the mission to the Gentiles coming to a head when Jewish Christians from Jerusalem came to Antioch and told the Greeks who had been baptized by Paul and Barnabas, "Unless you are circumcised according to the Mosaic practice, you cannot be saved" (Acts 15:1). This doubtless threw the Gentile Christian community into confusion, so Paul and Barnabas headed a delegation to Jerusalem to seek a clarification. The "apostles and presbyters" were convened to discuss the matter. Peter, Paul, and Barnabas told of their experiences, and Peter argued that God had shown his approval of the incorporation of the Gentiles without requiring Jewish observance "by granting them the holy Spirit just as he did us" (15:8). James, the "brother of the Lord," the acknowledged leader of the Jewish Christians, agreed with Peter (using the Hebrew form of his name, Symeon, in verse 14), and that swayed the decision in favor of an uninhibited Gentile mission.

The council composed a letter to communicate the decision to the Greek Christians in Antioch and sent it with Paul and Barnabas and special Jerusalem representatives Judas and Silas. There was great rejoicing in Antioch, and after a time Judas and Silas returned to Jerusalem with greetings of peace to the community there, while "Paul and Barnabas remained in

Antioch, teaching and proclaiming with many others the word of the Lord" (15:35).

Now that a moment of peace had come, Paul thought that he and Barnabas should take the opportunity to return to the Greek communities they had evangelized to "see how the brothers are getting on" and to communicate to them the good news of the Jerusalem council's decision.

37Barnabas wanted to take with them also John, who was called Mark. 38But Paul insisted that they should not take with them someone who had deserted them at Pamphylia and who had not continued in their work. 39So sharp was their disagreement that they separated.

Luke does not reveal that Barnabas and Mark were cousins—that information comes from Colossians 4:10—but the family relationship is supported by the way Barnabas interacts with Mark in Acts. We know that Mark's mother Mary lived in Jerusalem (Acts 12:12), and very likely Mark, a young man, lived with her. Barnabas and Saul had visited Jerusalem on a relief mission shortly before beginning the mission to Cyprus, and soon afterward Mark went with them "as their assistant" (Acts 13:5), so they had probably visited Mary's home during their stay. Cyprus was a safe place for Barnabas and Saul to begin their evangelizing venture, since it was home territory to Barnabas. If Mark was Barnabas' cousin, it would have been home territory for Mark, too, in the sense that his grandparents and other relatives were there; and that would also explain why his mother would have given permission for the bold overseas trip.

When the Cyprus mission was successful and the missionaries gained some confidence, it seemed like a good idea to continue the journey into Pamphylia and break new ground for the Gospel. At this point, Mark returned to Jerusalem, and Paul interpreted this as desertion of the mission. He thought Mark had forfeited his right to go with them again.

When has a fuller understanding of circumstances prevented discord or division? How willing are you to listen for the fuller story?

But there may have been another side and Barnabas, the son of encouragement, would have been more likely to know about it than the fiery Paul, who was not famous for patient listening. Barnabas may have known—and may have tried to explain to Paul—that young Mark was worried that he didn't have permission from his mother to go beyond Cyprus, which had already been a notable concession. Paul jumped to the conclusion that Mark was deserting the mission, but Mark may only have been doing what he felt obedience to his mother required.

This would also explain Barnabas' sharp reaction when Paul wouldn't let Mark go with them this second time. We are a bit uneasy to see Barnabas in a quarrel. Everywhere else he has been cooperative, humble, seeking the good of others before his own. It's not difficult to visualize Paul in a sharp disagreement, but it is harder to imagine Barnabas in such a scene. But if Barnabas considered Paul's treatment of Mark an injustice, it would be consistent with Barnabas' character for him to stand up for the one mistreated. We haven't seen him concerned with a slight or inconvenience to himself, but when he perceived injustice to another, he was aroused. He was gentle, but not a milquetoast.

What have you learned from life and from Scripture about standing up for others *and* about the power of gentleness?

39Barnabas took Mark and sailed to Cyprus.
40But Paul chose Silas and departed after being commended by the brothers to the grace of the Lord.

We don't hear anything more about Barnabas in the Acts of the Apostles. From now on, the narrative will follow the career of Paul: his preaching missions, his arrest in Jerusalem, and his journey to Rome, where, though under house arrest, at the end of Acts he preaches about the kingdom of God and the Lord Jesus Christ "with complete assurance and without hindrance" (Acts 28:31). On the way, Paul will link up with other disciples besides Silas, prominently Timothy, Priscilla and Aquila, and maybe even Luke himself, if that is what is indicated by a series of so-called "we passages" beginning with the change in Acts 16:11, where the narrator says, "We set sail from Troas, making a straight run for Samothrace."

Meanwhile, Barnabas took Mark to Cyprus, probably for a preaching mission that combined a family visit. But soon after that, as we know from Paul's report in Galatians, Barnabas was

back at Antioch when Paul confronted Peter for not eating with the Gentile Christians when he visited Antioch after the Council of Jerusalem (Gal 2:11-14). Barnabas is here accused of siding with Peter and the other Jerusalem visitors and being "carried away by their hypocrisy" (v. 13).

But we have only Paul's side of the issue, and Peter and Barnabas may have had another way of looking at it. The acceptance of Gentiles into the church was a sore point for the conservative Jewish Christian party in Jerusalem. That some of the Jerusalem group had come to Antioch with Peter may indicate that they were willing to take a step of reconciliation, and Peter may have wanted them to feel at ease in Antioch before he brought the two groups together.

A few years after this, Paul would write to the Corinthians defending his own similar conduct: "I have made myself a slave to all so as to win over as many as possible. To the Jews I became like a Jew to win over Jews; to those under the law I became like one under the law—though I myself am not under the law—to win over those under the law" (1 Cor 9:19-20). This was exactly the kind of conduct he was condemning in Peter and Barnabas at Antioch. Obviously, he had changed his approach in the meantime. Maybe he had learned from them!

A few verses earlier in the same letter to the Corinthians, Paul aligns himself with Barnabas when responding to attacks on his apostleship and on his conduct of the ministry (1 Cor 9:1-12). The accusation was that, unlike other apostles, Paul did not take advantage of the right to be supported by the community he served. Because he continued to do other work to support himself (though he would accept help from some communities: see Phil 4:15-18), critics said this proved he wasn't a true apostle. Paul gives several reasons why he has the right to support from the communities he serves, but goes on to say he doesn't use that privilege in order to avoid harm to the gospel ministry. Apparently there had been charlatans who had caused scandal and taken advantage of the fledgling Christian communities. In support of his manner of exercising apostleship, Paul invokes the example of Barnabas, who had adopted the same approach that he had.

Barnabas is described as a man for others. Who do you know who exhibits a similar desire to serve the needs of the church?

The writing of Paul's First Letter to the Corinthians is usually dated to shortly before Pentecost in the year 57. The positive mention of Barnabas as Paul's coworker in the ministry at this point indicates that all hard feelings from the earlier disagreement have dissipated. If they have for Paul, we can be sure they have for Barnabas, who was interested only in what was good for the ministry, regardless of what it meant for himself. He was a man for others at the heart of the early church. Without his humility, persistence, and grace, we might not have had Paul for the work of the Gospel, and we can only imagine the loss for the church. Once Paul was in the ministry, Barnabas did everything he could, without compromising principle, to support and promote him as he did everyone else. Words of Jesus quoted earlier by Luke could serve as a portrait of Barnabas: "[L]et the greatest among you be as the youngest, and the leader as the servant" (Luke 22:26).

Praying the Word / Sacred Reading

The early followers of Jesus did not hide their disagreements in the interest of leaving a pristine witness for later generations. Their disagreements were genuine and their conversations frank. The evidence eventually emerges that over time the differing parties do not remain at odds. The church is made stronger in reconciling.

Take time in prayer to acknowledge the differing viewpoints and experiences that exist in our parishes today, and in the broader church. How are you being called to speak honestly? And how can your speech and actions always remain open to the needs of the Body of Christ?

Spend some time speaking honestly to God about situations of strife within the church. And be prepared to listen for God's voice.

Living the Word

Reexamine your role in any disagreements among God's faithful. Consider to what extent your views are motivated by self-interest or hurt feelings and to what extent they are motivated by your care for the community's health and wholeness. Resolve to work toward a genuine resolution, taking Barnabas as your example.